# Through the Square Window

SINÉAD MORRISSEY was born in 1972 and grew up in Belfast. She is the author of three previous collections: *There Was Fire in Vancouver* (1996), *Between Here and There* (2002) and *The State of the Prisons* (2005). Her awards include the Patrick Kavanagh Award, an Eric Gregory Award, the Rupert and Eithne Strong Award and the Michael Hartnett Poetry Prize. *The State of the Prisons* was a Poetry Book Society Recommendation and both *Between Here and There* and *The State of the Prisons* were shortlisted for the T.S. Eliot Prize. *The State of the Prisons* was also shortlisted for the *Irish Times* Poetry Prize and the John Llewellyn Rhys Commonwealth Literature Prize. In 2007 she received a Lannan Literary Fellowship. Her poem 'Through the Square Window' was awarded first place in the UK National Poetry Competition the same year. Sinéad Morrissey is lecturer in creative writing at the Seamus Heaney Centre for Poetry, Queen's University, Belfast.

Also by Sinéad Morrissey from Carcanet Press

*There Was Fire in Vancouver*
*Between Here and There*
*The State of the Prisons*

First published in Great Britain in 2009 by

Carcanet Press Limited
Alliance House
Cross Street
Manchester M2 7AQ

Copyright © Sinéad Morrissey 2009

A CIP catalogue record for this book is available from the British Library
ISBN 978 1 84777 057 8

The publisher acknowledges financial assistance from Arts Council
England

Typeset by XL Publishing Services, Tiverton
Printed and bound in England by SRP Ltd, Exeter

SINÉAD MORRISSEY

# *Through the Square Window*

**CARCANET**

*for Augustine*

# Acknowledgements

Acknowledgements are due to the editors of the following publications in which some of these poems have previously appeared: *A Fine Statement* (Poolbeg, 2008), *Circa Art Magazine*, *The Independent on Sunday*, *New Hibernia Review*, *New Welsh Review*, *Poetry London*, *PN Review*, *Poetry Review*, *The Stinging Fly*, *The Ulster Tatler* and *The Yellow Nib*.

'Cycling at Sea Level' was written for inclusion in *From the Small Back Room: A Festschrift for Ciaran Carson* (Netherlea Press, 2008). 'Electric Edwardians' was written for inclusion in *Love Poet, Carpenter: for Michael Longley at 70* (Enitharmon Press, 2009). 'The Invitation' was written in response to the art of Benjamin de Burca and commissioned by the Irish Arts Council, *The Stinging Fly* and *Circa Art Magazine*.

Thanks are due to the committee and staff of Chateau Lavigny, Switzerland, for a writing residency in the summer of 2006.

I gratefully acknowledge the receipt of a Lannan Literary Fellowship in November 2007.

# Contents

## Storm

It was already Gothic
enough, what with that
King-of-Versailles-sized bed
with room for me and two
or three liveried footmen;

wall-lights like candle-shafts
in fake pearl and cut
glass; and the stranded
little girl in the photographs
growing sorrowful—

her cascade sleeves, her floral
crown—as though taken
by Lewis Carroll. All afternoon
the church bells rang out
their warning. Cumulostratus

ascended into heaven.
Evening and the white forked
parting of the sky fell
directly overhead, casements
rattled on hinges and Thunder

may as well have summoned
the raggle-taggle denizens
of his vociferous world:
the ghouls, the gashed, the dead
so bored by now of being

dead they flock to gawk—
sanctuary was still sanctuary
except more so, with the inside
holding flickeringly, and the
outside clamouring in.

# Saint-Exupéry

That the world might be burnt clean by gasoline
exploding in an engine, was completely unforeseen
by Saint-Exupéry, who, after his aeroplane crashed
in the Sahara, saw his former self evaporate like mist—

leaving a thirst like acid on the tongue,
snakes, sun, rocks, and the hypnagogic vision
of a tyrannous, golden prince, whom he rendered later
with blackened eyes like thumbprints off a newspaper.

# A Device for Monitoring Brain Activity by Shining Light into the Pupil

*after Petr Borkovec*

A liner in the foreground of the Lough
—dead-centre but already passing on—
white as a tent in Plantagenet France. I walked
the steep road to the shore, which tips
the earth into ocean,
levers ocean up to heaven,
as though broken in the middle by a hand.
I watched for gulls where the Threemilewater
empties and spills. The liner shone.

Ducks were tugging each other out to sea.
They rode each wave the liner sent
percussively. They wobbled and re-gathered
in the succeeding calm. Across the Lough
—if only for a moment—hillsides
snided in gorse bushes crackled and sang.
A straggle of crows, backs to the enemy,
were guarding the bars fencing the cenotaph
while cormorants out on the platform—

huddled and avuncular and jet-dark
as obsidian—were as standing stones
to the wash beneath them: the tide
advanced, the water glistening.

Smashed mussel shells banked
against the sides of rocks burned blue
in the sun. And though the waves from the ship
still repeated along the bulwark, decreasing
in intensity, the door to the sea floor stood open
in between: sand, weeds, a trolley
taking several hundred years to disappear.
Light fell unequally at the horizon's vanishing-
point as though the edge of the world glared upwards.

The liner shone all the while.
Absorbing the sunlight, throwing it out again.
That shimmering, regal tent, I thought,
is almost like a ship: complete with passengers
and a captain's banquet. It could be that.
Brightness blurred the skin of everything.
I watched the gulls flare white
above the river mouth and saw, in hours,
how their wings, to a still-blue sky, would answer black.

# Matter

*for S.P.*

Aristotle observed and recorded it all—
that out of rainwater, the marrow
of the human spine, foam from the sea,
or the putrefying carcasses of bulls and horses
spring living beings: frogs, serpents, anchovies,
bees and scarabs, locusts, weevils, maggots.
St Augustine agreed: what matter that the smallest
(and most meddlesome) of God's creatures
find no mention in the chronicle of the Ark?
So long as alluvial mud remained, or rotted
wood, or rinsed white bones of crocodiles
after the wash abated and the salvaged couple
and their braying entourage were pitched
on top of Ararat, wasps and gnats and fleas
would manifest once more in clouds and colonies
without a union of the sexes (like Mary)
and the earth would effortlessly teem.
Recipes for rats and 'small white puppies
a child might play with' followed
during the Middle Ages, which typically included
hay, excrement, dirty shirts, wool
simmered for an hour then hung to dry
in an outhouse or chicken coop
(the air of such places being itself
so mutable and laden with infusoria,
it acts as a bridge to life). Golems
moulded from clay still needed a spell
to keep them animated, as though by
growing bigger and more complicated,
the offspring of the elements
were in danger of winding down,
yet Paracelsus, arch-advocate of decay,
saw no reason not to apply
the laws of spontaneous generation
to ourselves: *let the semen of a man*
*putrefy by itself for forty days in a sealed*

*cucurbite, it shall begin, at last, to live.*
Fed on an arcanum of human blood
and kept in darkness, his fleet homunculus
had all the features of a human child.
Leeuwenhoek bore this experiment in mind
when, decades later, using his own microscope,
he scrutinised his sperm, magnified
as much as three hundred times and fashioned
like a bell, with the wrought perfection
of a tiny man curled inside each globule.
Ovists may have envisaged instead
a sacred cabinet of children, encased
inside each egg, opening in time
both backwards and forwards
to the breaking of Eve and the End
of the World, the likelihood remained:
whether one believed in this, or the evidence
of a light-blanched workshop and a knack
for polished glass, or whether one went back
to what the Greeks expressed
as the facts of reproduction,
a woman's quest for contraception,
stacked against the odds of dogged visitors
finding lodging in the womb
at any beckoning, was hopeless.
No wonder Soranus suggested water from blacksmiths'.
No wonder olive oil, the pulp of a pomegranate,
honey, pine resin, mercury, beeswax,
pennyroyal, tobacco juice, arrowroot, tansy
were burnt, brewed, inhaled, ingested,
inserted into the cervix, or buried in fields left fallow
if the coppery stain of menstruation
persisted into the seventh day.
No wonder witches consulted the sky.
And though I know, thanks in part to Pasteur—
to his gauze impediments and penchant
for boiling—how you came to enter,
how you came to roll and hiccup and kick
against the windowless dark, feet to my heart
and skull to the pelvic cradle, I still think
of our lovemaking as a kind of door
to wherever you were, waiting in matter,

spooled into a form I have not yet been shown
by the unprompted action of nature,
by something corrupting in an earthenware pot
in Corinth, say, or Kingstown.
Stay the wind on a river eight weeks after equinox—
witness blue-green mayflies lift off
like a shaken blanket; add algae
and alchemical stones to the lake floor
in the strengthening teeth of winter, what swans.

# The Reversal

*I cannot rub the strangeness from my sight*
*I got from looking through a pane of glass*
*I skimmed this morning from the drinking trough…*

Robert Frost

The lake, laid flat again, sloshes and jerks
to a cat-lapped equilibrium.
At sunset, its surface is alive with flies.

There are more otters than wide-mouthed bass.
There are more lightning-struck trees
than otters: singed palisades

of the backwaters, where a small stream
pierces the interior and the bones
of the bulrushes have set down their bells.

Paucity in the rainy season—
children people the floating piers
and tally their tiny catches

until a flush moon afloat out of nowhere
drives them inside. They and the hornet moths
and the skinny Apache crows

and the after-supper men leaning over
on their porches by the furred lamps
smoking their cigarettes

are unperturbed at the prospect
of reversal's return: that the lake
will be breathed on, its meniscus frozen,

then its whole top skimmed off
and lifted high—
the way a man might peer into a barrel

and glimpse in its icecap
a monocle; the way
rain and fire and the sea broke laws in Egypt.

# Returning from Arizona

Back from the kiln-fired punishment of Mars
        where humans cannot live
        except indoors or in air-conditioned cars
and roadside shrines show Jesus in his crib

with a black face even in summer,
        our plane descends
        through a vapourish downpour:
the now-usual August deluge of these islands.

Rain smears the windows. Rivers have overshot
        their mark and fields
        for miles around the airport
sport pewter lakes. A heron stands by a cattle shed.

Getting too much of what you've acutely missed
        too suddenly
        —the median notion botched—
can render you wary of wishing's blunt chicanery:

like longing for weeks to be sick
        to prove the baby's taken,
        then failing to find a tonic
for another being's foothold in your person.

# Found Architecture

*for Kerry Hardie*

These days are all about waiting. What would you say
if I tried to explain how my single true activity
this wet and shivery May is 'found architecture'?

As the giver of an Italian kaleidoscope
that makes its heel-toe shapes, not from beads or seeds
or painted meticulous details, but from the room,

from whatever room I happen to be in,
or from the street, always eager and unerringly
democratic, you stand slightly to the south of me

with your head raised and I imagine you smiling.
The day it arrived I mangled the blue of the bathroom
with the pistachio green of my bedroom ceiling

and sat entranced: such symmetrical splicing
of everything, anything, to make of my waiting-house
a star-pointed frame that entered and left

itself behind as the cylinder turned. Any light that there was
was instantly mystical—a crack in the pattern's
typography, like the door at the end of the corridor

shedding radiance. Yesterday evening, by the sea,
a strangled sealed-off swamp by a walkway
threw up, suddenly, the Aboriginal outback:

rotted glands of a pond between knee-high grasses
and a white tree undoing itself in its ink-stained
surfaces. The tree looked like a crocodile's ribcage

as I passed along the perimeter, or the wide-propped
jawbone of a whale. Until it became, the further
I walked, a canoe, asleep on the water and fettered

with algae. Another dead branch sat up
in the grass like the head of an otter and talked.
This, too, was found architecture. And all the usual,

of course: skeletons of geranium leaves on windowsills
long afterwards; snakeskins, clouds.
Beaches are full of it: found architecture being

the very business of beaches. Most recently
(and most disarmingly) this: handed to me in a roll
of four like mug-shot photographs from a machine—

his seahorse spine, his open-shut anemone
of a heart, and the row of unbelievable teeth
shining high in the crook of his skull as though backstitched

into place. From blood and the body's
inconsolable hunger I have been my own kaleidoscope—
five winter-bleached girls on a diving board, ready to jump.

# Vanity Fair

Dearest William—

I could begin by hoping you are well in England
(and I do!) now that the ——th regiment has returned
to Chatham; or I could begin by telling you
that reports of worsening weather here are true;
that Georgie thinks you wicked and unkind
for leaving him; that your former servants pine;
or that father, though no better, is no worse, etc.
But this is not a weather-talk sort of letter.
It is after three. The whole house sleeps
(even Becky) and I am kept awake six weeks
by your crippling absence: an irony, I confess,
since for all your years of passionate presence
I failed to cherish you… Now that you're gone,
Becky (and you were right about her all along)
keeps dreadful company: boorish men who jest
and drink and flirt and she isn't in the slightest
shocked by any of it. I keep to my room.
I have placed the portrait of George face down
on the dresser. I have folded the gloves you left
in an innermost drawer, as though they were a gift.
Since you spoke of my *incapacity* for love
I have come to see how my own fierce widowhood
was a shell against the world, a kind of carapace
made up of pride, stupidity and cowardice,
a stay, if you will, against 'the kind of attachment'
such as yours for me deserved. Poor shredded raiment—
for if it did not keep me warm, it kept me safe,
safe against you and safe against myself.
Last year, at the opera (it was *Dido and Aeneas*),
I wished to take your hand—in a sudden, artless,
harmless way that would not give you pause—
then didn't. I think I must have sensed the charge
built up from a decade's loving in your fingers
(though there you sat, as solid as an anchor)
and feared that touching it would knock me flat.
Now I'm scared I shall die without it.

Dear Dobbin, come back. Like everything else we do
in our mingled, muddy lives, this letter is overdue.
Forgive me if my love arrives belatedly,
but there is a ship can get you here by Friday
and, come all the rain in Christendom,
I shall be waiting for you by the viewing platform.
Dearest William, put out to sea.

Yours, Amelia Sedley.

## Cycling at Sea Level

Because weather's variation plays differently each day
(forgetfulness being a condition of peace)
I'm cycling home along the Lagan as it empties into the Lough

with only the wind to slow my flickering telegraph.
My wheels make a noise like ticker tape.
The Gasworks. The Chinese Bridge. Our Squares of Hope. The Fish—

to Duncrue Industrial Estate whose meat-
plant and meal-factory have threaded the air with dust—
to Belfast Dump's Shore Park: pure scooped brown earth and salt,

looking for all the world
as though some meteor hit and killed off half the planet...
The sun's an unimpeded circuitry that lights such trees along the
                                                    cycle path

they shine like saints, like knives,
where the river opens, one artery to another, to multiplying water.
How many possibilities in a deck of cards?

The same, but changed, the corrugated colours of the mudflats
have so arranged themselves this afternoon
I forget every previous journey home and reconfigure

history: a white yacht leans on the breeze;
a solitary bait-digger, booted to the thigh, is casting a shadow
                                                    long enough
to hoist him up by.

Something is unravelling from the bolted-down telescopes
that line the Whitehouse wall, that offer a view of the moon
          or a stranded whale,
and I don't know what it is:

this single moment framed, what passes under a wheel's
                                                    circumference,
or the curlew's vanishing question in the sand:
*for me, for me, for me?*

# Apocrypha

When I was ten and convinced
I would never have children

simply by keeping my underwear on
at night-time, I was disarmed

by the history
of Mary Ann Sexton—

mother, camp-follower, picker
of pockets, stower of teeth—

and of how her womb
was pierced by a bullet

still wet from the testicle
of a Roundhead Lieutenant

at the Battle of Marston Moor.
As though the slaughter itself

required climax and sought out
the unlikeliest agents, or

a new king pined
to be born, this was as improbable

a conception
as the physical laws of the earth

and all the revolving planets
could allow.

What hope was underwear now?
If destiny hovered

with green wings and a stained,
indefatigable purpose

over my bedspread,
I, too, would be done for.

# Ice

They've come & gone before.
      Two hours or so
of a fine rain freezing on impact
      & what passes
for the world in West Quebec
      (woods, sugar-
bush, pylons, sheep) has spangled
      itself in ice.
Branches bend & snap & forests
      for years afterwards
hold their grieving centres bare
      where Pin Oak,
Siberian Elm, Common Hackberry
      & Bradford Pear
perform a shorn prostration & are
      unable to right
themselves; they teach the weeping
      willow how it's
done. Sometimes Frost's broken
      dome of heaven
is how storms end, just that, a shattering
      in the sunlight
of the million crystal filaments
      that fell & hung
on everything, as though absence of
      breath had caused
the general lock-in & simple breath
      was all we ever
needed to un-sleeve the present
      & make it real again.

\*

Monday, January 5th: we wake
        to a bluish light
lasering through the window, a wiped
        display on the radio
& the racket of gunshot. The house
        is cold & all
around the trees are coming down.
        First the crack
at the stem of the weight-sore trunk,
        then a clinking
magnified, a china shop upending
        in an earthquake,
as the branches rattle & snag.
        When the whole
tree hits, a volley of shots goes up
        & its burden of glass
explodes. This ten, twenty, fifty times
        until we lose each crash
to the cacophony of the week-long storm.
        I still remember
you standing in your housecoat
        that first night
& how your face was lit by the
        transformer
shorting out outside. We didn't know
        the blackout
ended five states wide, or that the
        footprint
of the ice-storm could be seen
        from space.


                        *

The sheep were dead. The summary
        execution
of every maple within earshot
        finally stopped
at dawn on the penultimate day.
        The house still
stood, astonished, the one upright
        among a litter
of horizontals, & while it rained
        & froze, rained
& froze, a quiet inside the rainfall
        began to
spread itself abroad, all targets down,
        all debris blown
asunder. You begged me to check
        the sheep.
I knew before I reached them two
        hours later—
the outline of my person hanging
        frozen in the air—
that none of them had survived.
        The silence
was ubiquitous & pure as star-silence.
        So all I had
to offer as I slipped & slithered home-
        wards was an out-
building of kneeling, petrified sheep,
        locked to their
spots like pieces in a Snow Queen's
        game of chess.


                    *

Frost flowers. Bearded trees. Ghosts
      of some sudden
deleterious fungus ballooning out
      of the brushwood
one spectacular rose-bowl morning
      the previous
fall. The lavish, sexual freeze
      of long-stemmed
plants whose ensuing ersatz petals
      splinter when
touched. Midnight, January 9th:
      the jettisoned
excess of the Mississippi Delta
      had punished
us enough. Rain reverted to gas. Before
      the burials, before
the muddy thaw, before the gathering
      mass of melted ice
flooded the south, before the army
      & the extraction
of what was felled from what was
      left, we stood
at our living-room window & watched
      a tiny moon
& a tatter of stars high up in the
      atmosphere
& kissed as two will kiss through sheets
      dipped in dis-
infectant, & everything between us
      flew apart.

\*

## 'Love, the nightwatch…'

Love, the nightwatch, gloved and gowned, attended.
Your father held my hand. His hands grew bruised
and for days afterwards wore a green and purple coverlet

when he held you to the light, held your delicate, dented
head, thumbed-in like a water font. They used
stopwatches, clip charts, the distant hoof beats of a heart

(divined, it seemed, by radio, so your call fell intertwined
with taxicabs, police reports, the weather blowing showery
from the north) and a beautiful fine white cane,

carved into a fish hook. I was a haystack the children climbed
and ruined, collapsing almost imperceptibly
at first, then caving in spectacularly as you stuttered and came

—crook-shouldered, blue, believable, beyond me—
in a thunder of blood, in a flood-plain of intimate stains.

# Missing Winter

The clocks have been set back
and suddenly morning
is safeguarded again:
birds on the Lough
like guests at a wedding.

Though the four o'clock dark
is massed, obliterating—
winter come careening
in storms over the Shore Park,
its hair undone and the back door banging.

Last year I missed this slippage
completely: five weeks in
to our botched conversation
of doorways and diptychs, of wreckage,
of howling, and he unknown,

his arrival so fast,
his skin had been lost
in transit, tossed off
in an anteroom of umbrellas and hats
like the overnight pupation of the gypsy moth.

He had to re-grow it,
moon-ring by moon-ring;
his intestine spasmed on everything
fed to him… That bathtub light,
the plug hauled out and draining

a whole hour sooner
than expected, contained within its glint and grain
one singular disastrous kitchen,
a screaming boy abandoned on the floor,
and me, no longer listening,

but thinking instead of storks—
land-herons, monogamists,
as attached to their rooftop nests
as to their partners, legs like two forks
trailing in a headwind and blessed,

above all creatures, with sex—
and I wished the stork back,
with its bundle-used beak
and impossible kindnesses—
I wished the stork back.

# Augustine Sleeping Before He Can Talk

The only places he can dive to are the senses.
The Christmas lights his father dangled from the corners
of his ceiling in July are his palimpsest for the world—
a winking on and off of ebullient colour, unnamed and so untamed,
to be committed to memory and then written over.
For now the world is simply to be crawled into, like the sea,
of which he has no fear, a bubbling, transmogrifying, all-
attracting mechanism that has not yet disappointed
with the mean-spirited vanishing act of an ink-black horizon.
He has already learned how the tongue contains more mystery
than the granite hulk of an elephant swaying suddenly into focus
under the dank and knotted overhang of Cave Hill, tossing
straw onto its shoulders to keep itself warm because it still
—and tragically—remembers Africa, that when he opens
his mouth to admit the spoon, anything can happen,
from passion fruit to parmesan. The three tributary-
sounds of his name that flow as one (as though summer's
hottest month had a feminine ending) he knows, and the purring
of cats and cars and the howling of dogs and fireworks.
His fingers adjust the tufts of the sheepswool coat
he lies on in his sleep. Tomorrow I'll offer him the dent
of a worry stone and the fluted sticky centres of acacia flowers.
All this can only be where he goes—there can be no other possibility—
unless we accept that memory begins in the womb or back,
still further, in the undiscovered bourne poor Hamlet dreamed
of entering without map or compass as a deliverance
from the sight of our back garden in September, the apple tree
keeled over and cankered and the fuchsia disrobed.
If he ever bombs inside a swimming-pool, or deep-sea dives,
or moon-walks, if he ever moves from balancing
on some underwater floor, precariously filled with air,
to pressing off on the balls of his feet into his own ascent,
through a dense and illegible element, he may remember
what it felt like to wake when he was one, and that it was
a slow, alert surfacing towards the morning, the clock's face,
the seagulls and the sea's address, all clamouring to be experienced.

# Through the Square Window

In my dream the dead have arrived
to wash the windows of my house.
There are no blinds to shut them out with.

The clouds above the Lough are stacked
like the clouds are stacked above Delft.
They have the glutted look of clouds over water.

The heads of the dead are huge. I wonder
if it's my son they're after, his
effortless breath, his ribbon of years—

but he sleeps on unregarded in his cot,
inured, it would seem, quite naturally
to the sluicing and battering and paring back of glass

that delivers this shining exterior…
One blue boy holds a rag in his teeth
between panes like a conjuror.

And then, as suddenly as they came, they go.
And there is a horizon
from which only the clouds stare in,

the massed canopies of Hazelbank,
the severed tip of the Strangford Peninsula,
and a density in the room I find it difficult to breathe in

until I wake, flat on my back with a cork
in my mouth, bottle-stoppered, in fact,
like a herbalist's cure for dropsy.

# The Invitation

*for/after Benjamin de Burca*

I

You think you're safe? You think all this can stay?
The solid success of a high-banked fire, a February at bay
beyond the window? Put down your book. Take off your watch.
Empty your pockets. The single thing to catch
as the fault-line under the armchair begins its torn
pronouncement—a hairline crack that opens,
imperceptibly, to a drought-impacted tracery embedded in the
                                                    floorboards—
as the gathering chatter of screens, dishes, silverware, drawers
sounds out a secret language, a scornful chorus—
is the light. That wintry, five o'clock light. Its emptying grace.
Note how the western quadrant of the sky has taken the organ
of the swallowed sun and made it more, in absence, than it was at
                                                    noon.
Note how the clouds turn black in advance of night. As both
                                                    afterthought
and prophecy, light persists or vanishes and all hard-fought
expectations are defied. Note too how daylight's posthumous flare
depends upon its opposite; how kind to colour dark's
                                    encroachments are...
A hole, a portal, is opening at your feet as the mantelpiece collapses
and a linen closet hurtles down the stairs. Your living-room has an
                                                    axis
you never knew existed and its sudden revolution sees you
                                    witless, stumped.
Take light's sure paradoxes with you. Jump.

Circles within circles. And here's another riddle straightaway:
that absolute black can have a blacker heart, a glistening thigh
lodged within its centre. You're plummeting within a lift-
shaft, darker, glossier, than either the rabbit-hole or well
                                        surrounding it.
The landing knocks you out. How long? You wake to birdsong.
A nineteenth-century farmyard. The intimation of a building.
Perhaps it's morning—what light there is is surely compromised
                                        —or dusk.
And then you see: you've landed in the shadowland of some
                                        bizarre eclipse
where blackness reigns in patches. Night falls at random, divided
     from the sky:
darkness turned autonomous, in love with its own wild deft
                                        capacity
to take light's definition of each working day and render it senseless.
There should be implements here: a plough, a pitchfork, chickens,
                                        horses—
a context. Wipe out the pool and the six-year-old Narcissus, in love
with his own reflection, looks shot and left to die. Cover
the earth and the pious farmhand, welded to his pick,
is trapped afresh in labour, in Capital's obliterating logic.
And there is no bleed between. Stationed above a bowl of black
it cannot hope to soften, unpierced by leaves, unballasted by tracks,
carts, hedges or hostelry, a five o'clock sky, mindful of nothing
but its own rejoicing, is teaching itself to sing.

Who am I? You've met me twice before. Once in Tanigumi, Japan;
once in Amsterdam. The gate to Tanigumi's oldest shrine
had the shoes of a thousand pilgrims nailed into its beams.
And by the avenue leading up to it, recessed in the trees,
on a moribund Shinto altar, the statue of a fox.
O tricksterish deity! How the reek of untamed mischief rose off
its flanks like steam. The Reichsmuseum's *Menacing Cupid*
revealed me a second time: my body succulent, my arrow sure,
now I had

the alabaster features of a glowering boy, abrim with wry intention…
Cupid, Trickster, Fox, Love's Cursor, The-Boy-Who-Fell-Under-
the-Hay-Wain
and-Lived-to-Tell-the-Tale, I am the Maria at midnight, the wind
at sea,

the accident waiting to happen, I am what cannot be appeased
by wine, rice cakes, prayer, entreaty, I am what cannot be undone.
Let's say (it's easiest) that this is all a dream: the partial farmyard
scene;

the laws of day and night suspended; the drinking corpse…
Let's catapult you back up through the lift shaft to your waiting
space

beneath the window. The floor is smooth again. The crockery at
peace.

Yet something strange will stay. Remember Alice?
*Toothscomb—Fury—Ambleweed—Frost—*
Once broken through, a permeable membrane gives at the
slightest touch.

# Townhouse

These are our spell-safe days.
Before my mother dies, I inhabit a three-storey house
and exist, for the most part, on the middle floor.

There is the view of the sea
—dependable in its leave-taking—
there is the shunted garden we have tried to fix

with shells and summer's eponymous flowers.
We have accomplished the trick
of a child, who, in this staircased space,

has been taking the wheel of speech
into his mouth
then letting it go

to test its new circumference.
The attic is a reliquary
for the words my son will speak

when the arctic fox is lost
in snowmelt
and my father too long dead to stop it happening.

# Prayer Plant

It was given to me small, whorled like my brother's tongue
in the game when we were children, its three leaves
wrapped up tight in themselves, barred as an oyster.

I can scarcely remember what happened in between:
how many months (or pots) it took to enter
its own abundance. Now it hangs full and excitable

over my fireplace, concerned mostly with maintenance.
Come morning, after I've moved all night from room
to room in search of sleep, I can sometimes witness it

lower its fringe of adjustable oars beneath the rim
of its lazuli bowl, as though blushing, or weeping.
Then, by evening, before the sky has acknowledged that

—already—the light is draining, I catch it levering
its slow arms towards heaven again, mindful as Islam.
Is it praying in the dark or in the daytime?

# The Clangers

*for Gerald Boyle*

This planet, this cloudy planet, is the earth.
We cannot guess how flawed and insignificant it is
unless we travel, in our imaginations, to another star—
to another stone-pocked sphere without atmosphere
where an orderly people, curious and conciliatory,
stares out across the vast and silent territory
of intergalactic space, dreaming of otherness...

...which arrived, once,
in the shape of an iron chicken
they cobbled together from sky detritus.
It couldn't understand its own coordinates
and blundered all over the meteor garden
until Tiny Clanger—*there now there*—
calmed it into submission like a horse whisperer.
As thanks it laid an iron egg before flapping away
to its spiky nest. The egg was filled with staves
which Tiny Clanger planted and watched turn into music trees.

On other star-bright days, when otherness
fails to visit them, the Clangers resort to flying machines
to snatch whatever passing implement or instrument they can.
Flying machines are Major Clanger's passion.
It is the randomness of sky-fishing that excites him:
a functioning television set or a hat with live inhabitants—
whatever the harvest is, it must be clamorously exhibited
for the benefit of everyone, then taken
on a trolley to the Soup Dragon.

Inside the Clanger planet
there are caves and caves and caves full of flowers
and only the glow-buzzers know they are there at all.
Small Clanger got lost once, like all the countless dead before
                                        Theseus,
following the glow-buzzers to the glow-honey source.
At first he didn't notice: the caves an enticement of pearly lights

and unexpected airiness, the flowers a theatre.
While Granny Clanger nodded over her knitting
he was bowing to each extraordinary face in turn.
(Eventually, the glow-buzzers led him out again.)

Goodbye Clangers! That stretched and iridescent shawl
of stars and dark between your world and ours is beckoning…
Tuck yourselves into bed. Fold your ears over your eyes.
Whistle your singing-kettle breath one last time.

# York

The Plasterers: *The Creation*
The Cardmakers: *The Creation of Adam and Eve*

The Fullers: *Adam and Eve in Eden*
The Armourers: *The Expulsion*

The Shipwrights: *The Building of the Ark*
The Fishers and Mariners: *The Flood*

The Parchmentmakers and Bookbinders: *Abraham and Isaac*
The Pewterers and Founders: *Joseph's Trouble about Mary*

The Tilethatchers: *The Nativity*
St Leonard's Hospital: *The Purification*

The Vintners: *The Marriage at Cana*
The Cappers: *The Woman Taken in Adultery*

The Bakers: *The Last Supper*
The Cordwainers: *The Agony in the Garden and the Betrayal*

The Bowers and Fletchers: *Christ Before Annas and Caiaphas*
The Tapiters and Couchers: *The Dream of Pilate's Wife*

The Butchers: *The Death of Christ*
The Cooks and Waterleaders: *The Remorse of Judas*

The Tailors: *The Ascension*
The Potters: *Pentecost*

And episodes in between with a yet more fabulous cohabiting:
The Woolpackers and Woollenweavers: *The Assumption of the Virgin*

The Spurriers and Lorimers: *Christ and the Doctors*
The Spicers: *The Annunciation*, and

Because even a singing gash in the stratosphere is redeemable,
                                                    *The Fall of Man*
To the repairers of barrels, buckets, and tubs.

# History

Dear Heart, I dreamed a territory so seeming rich
and decorous, I woke with all its workings on my tongue.
Napoleon vanquished Europe. But when he died
(of natural causes) on the Palace-Garden Isle, Isola Bella,
built to resemble the rigging of ships, the map changed colour
from the Bay of Biscay to the Carpathian Peaks as bloodlessly
as the delicate octopus its rippling skin. The world shrugged off
his atheistic scarlet and dipped itself in yellow, the yellow of egg-
yolk and daylight's origin, and a Golden Age let down its iron bridge
and set us travelling. Everywhere was the same: commerce
was encouraged (though not excessively); order and cleanliness
governed and dignified both public and private realms; music
and poetry could be heard in all quarters. In Spain itself, the centre
of the Empire, all were as one: Language, Religion, the Crafts of State,
and the people flourished and were happy, the sap in the veins
of a Body Politick in rigorous health. Women, ever the lynchpin,
of households and families, of the men who bear the imperial
                                                            message
like a lamp into the dark, wore their mantle lightly, were softly
spoken, modestly attired, and though at liberty to work and roam
abroad, turned all their passion inwards to their sons and homes...

*Dear* Heart,

travelling through Switzerland in a previous summer, we stopped
in Berne and witnessed the *Zytglogge*: a medieval tower of time.
Beneath its east main face is an intricate astronomical and astrological
device, wherein, in one small radius, are displayed:
all twenty-four hours, the hours of brightness, the days
of the week, our position in the zodiac, the date, the month, the progress
of the moon and the degree of elevation of the sun on the horizon.
It was raining that straightforward, European rain we seldom see
at home and a small crowd murmured to their umbrellas
as Caspar Brunner's parade of bears, Chronos with his hourglass,
and a grinning jester in cap and bells rattled out of the darkness
four minutes to the hour. And my dream was like this—
as these eight signposts to our mortal existences
clicked and chimed together, so the interlocking arms

of God and Man and Government danced flawlessly there.
What measure of exactness could keep my golden territory
intact and accurate to the second? That same year, but later,
a woman read my fortune in a brace of cards. One showed a cup,
for love, and another a blinded girl, and another a hill of wheels
and gibbets, stood stark against the sky as the Saviour's Cross.

# Flu

When flu arrived that winter, I was ill for weeks.
Even my eyes were infected. I lay back and hallucinated—
the light was a flesh balloon; his face, when he came
with bitter effervescence, a bitten-through moon

or thigh bone…             After that, I slept
or stared at *A Century of Russian Photographs*.
Anastasia's chocolate frown. Lenin on his stack.
Lily Brik with her horseshoe teeth and headscarf.

And then page after page of unreadable scenes
I couldn't get the measure of, like the clusters of dots
in a magazine, containing a fortress
or Tyrannosaurus rex if you only knew how to lose focus.

The afternoons were quietest.
The streets outside my window held snow and letterboxes.

# Grammar

I look up from William Strunk's *Elements of Style*
and there it is: the river depositing ships
on the city's shimmering rim; the outsize girl
with her hoop; John Kindness's patchwork fish
with the docks in its sockets like a wash of oil.
My back has been turned so long I thought the whole
magnificent shebang had gone up protesting
in a pillar of smoke, but the faces on the train are real
as taxation and the sea-locked causeway is holding.
I read again: *do not join independent clauses*
*with a comma; the possessive of witness is witness's.*
How do you punctuate a soul in two places?
I leave half of it here, take half home to my son
with his bath accomplished and his sleepsuit on.

# The Innocents

*I've seen rooms used in broad daylight*
*as though they were dark woods—*

says Mrs Grose in a quavering voice;
the Governess holds her breath.

Anna has just been in to announce
that the children are washed

and waiting, ensconced
in their billowing cots upstairs,

their trio of candles flickering.
Their window is a window onto death.

In the kitchen, on the servants'
stairs, but mostly in the garden,

where the follies, statues, gazebos
and hedges clipped to the shapes

of birds and arches
stare on unappalled—

a pact is made. A beetle
crawls out of the mouth of a Cupid.

The Governess is right.
Little Flora giggles and plots.

All over the house, like the singeing
of the edges of the world

in autumn or the fraying
of chintz and lace, the roses

are undressing. Master Miles
lies considering his goodnight kiss.

## Mother Goose

None of it was real: the errant lambs, the crooked stiles,
the boys who seethed with snails and tails inside their pink exteriors
(though this, admittedly, made sense); nor that dyad of pitiful women,
Polly and Suki, held to ransom over the tea kettle.

Swallow a fly and the rest of the animal kingdom grows jealous.
Blow your horn and the moon—huge and sad and defencelessly
                                                    edible—
collapses into the cow paddock.

Still it goes on: on in that bashful exuberance of being five,
of non-sequiturs, of summer stretched
like a cradle of cats between the fingertips,
of summer preparing to turn the key in the lock and you not
                                                    noticing—

Lady, Lady, there's a hillside of handsome young men, pockets
spilling gold, selling tickets to London. They are expecting you.
Dizzy yourself by the mulberry bush. Grow your garden. Show
                                                    your shoe.

# Fairground Music

The fair had come. It must have been Whitsun.
They'd camp every year at the end of our yard—
you could hear the screams and the grinding of the rides
and a noise like whizz-bangs from the house.
Tom had taken Hazel off to get lost in it
so I had the kitchen to myself. Which was larger,
somehow, and scented, and lonely. I was baking scones.

It was Esther gave me the shock—*hello Doris*—
standing in the door-frame like a ghost.
She's been riding all afternoon: the dipper,
the dodgems, the giant wheel. You could tell
she was five months gone just by looking at her.
She needed the privy—*it would save me the walk*—
and I said alright because she was family.

She was out there an age. I had the scones in the oven
and the table scrubbed and the dishes washed
and draining on the rack and was wondering
if she'd stumbled on the garden path
when she came back, grey as a newspaper.
She put a hand to her hair and straightened her frock.
*See you at church, then. Give Tom my best*—

And then she left. I waited till the scones were finished,
dried my hands on a tea-towel, slipped my rings
from the windowsill, and made my way
past the rain barrel and the rabbit hutch to the door
of the outhouse, which was shut. Spiders' webs,
threaded like a lattice, covered the blistering paint.
I lifted the latch.

Inside, blood was everywhere: on the floor, on the walls.
You could tell where Esther had walked
by a set of white shadows. And then I saw her child—
bigger than the span of my hand and furred,
its fingers were curled near its ears and its eyelids were closed.
Its back was to the bowl. It was a girl.
I couldn't take my eyes off it, until I remembered

where I was and what had happened,
and stepped out onto the path and went back to the kitchen.
The sounds from the fair seemed louder
after that: hurdy gurdy music and the cries of the ticket sellers
ratcheting up for the evening...
I sat at the table, waiting for Tom to come in.
The ceiling caught the colours of the machines.

# Telegraph

Her father was born in Arkansas, the youngest, loneliest child
in a family of five. They lived in a four-roomed house
in a middle-sized town. When America went to war, he witnessed
columns of volunteers, filing out beyond the window,
singing, how fires on the street corners opposite blunted the night.
When his brothers got shot, he knew it was all his fault.

His mother was meticulous in punishment. So many faults
accrued to him, like interest, turning a fair-haired, freckled child
into a cross, she grew ingenious. If he wet the bed at night
(which he often did) she'd parade him through the house,
wrapped in a steaming sheet, to the frame of a backlit window,
so that people passing below might notice and be witness

to such wickedness. Other punishments went unwitnessed:
the confiscated meals, the bleeding feet. He was faulted
for speaking, and for keeping quiet. Mooning by the window
when his mother wasn't looking, he imagined himself a different child
in a different kind of country, Mexico perhaps, or Texas, in a house
that, barring moonlight, would be kept completely dark at night—

no standing lamps to shame him by… One night
while his parents slept, he ran away. There were no witnesses.
He left no note. He extracted himself from the house
like oil devolving itself from water, and found a job repairing faults
for the national telegraph company. Though still technically a child
(at seventeen) he knew this was his window

to the life he'd always dreamed of, a window
that would shut and lock before his twenty-first year. On a
                                        star-shot night
in Boulder, Colorado, he was married to Anne, who cried like a child,
while her father glowered beside them, their only witness.
The sex was her fault for being curious, the foetus her fault
that made her sick and saw them stuck in a four-roomed house

in a middle-sized town, so like the house
back home in Arkansas, his spirit failed him. Two small windows
stared onto the street. Anne grew silent, obedient to a fault.
Six months after the wedding, at ten past midnight,
Anne clutching the iron bedpost, the doctor arrived to witness
the birth of Mary Ruby Evans, their first and final child.

Whose fault that for twelve years afterwards in that house
a man slipped into the room of a child, kept back from the tiny
                                                    window,
and nightly undid what only the hawk moths witnessed?

## The Hanging Hare

Once, a boy
with a bare brown chest
brought a hare to our back door.
It was heavy summer: the alleyway
he walked along held August's
bin-lid stink & stupor.
He wouldn't stay,

declared the hare
a present from his father.
My brother fetched a length of string,
tied it by its feet, then watched as our mother
fastened it carefully to the iron banister
where it spun like the spiralling
seed of a sycamore,

losing momentum…
Soon enough it hung there
motionless, impaled upon its own
frozen direct line of perfect martyrdom,
its eye an abyss, its foxglove fur
unblemished bar the torn
& matted abdomen

where the shot
went in. I could have sat
at the foot of the flight of stairs
for hours to get the measure of it (its ear-tips
dipped in black against the almost-white
of its ears' interiors!) if my mother
had allowed it.

She banished me
outside, where the afternoon
lay festering, & yet it almost seemed as if
the sunken playground, hacked-out stumps of trees
& blackened mattresses where a fire had been
were wiped out by this gift,
this legacy

of unimpeded air,
of whitethorn-quartered fields
for miles around, of granular traces
still on the skin from a swimmable river,
of plovers' eggs, the calyx-wheels
of larkspur, of spaces
where a hare

might flourish…
Like a sideshow hawker
with a star exhibit, I rounded in
the street, before my father skinned & washed
& jugged the hare in blood & butter.
*Look*, I said to a ring of children
& pointed. *It's gorgeous.*

# Cathedral

As though the world were a spiral staircase,
and the order in which you ascended it
already set, I wanted the words
you attempted first to be solid and obvious:
*apple, finger, spoon.* The bat
hanging like a blister in your drool-proof
baby book or the lovesick cricket
with its gossamer instrument
were surely to be held back:
until I could explain, until I could build
you a zoo of improbable candidates
and properly introduce you.
But you were too quick—
like panic, there was no stopping it—
each day's vast, unbreachable
impact—and language,
in whatever ramshackle order
it made its presence felt—
a movable moon, the guts
of a clock, a fire escape—
rained down and into you, like
Catherine Linton's wine-through-water
dream of the heath and expulsion
from heaven. I cannot hang
a curtain to keep it off. I cannot
section it. It is entering via
the ear's aqueduct, every
listening second, trickling in
to its base equilibrium
and carrying with it an image in negative
to be absorbed by the brain and stored.
*Bah! humbug!* you say, aged two,
like the terrible man
in the cape with the walking stick
you glimpsed in the afternoon,
and what we assumed you knew
is jolted on its axis; then this:
*at six o'clock the ghost
of a child might come and eat porridge.*
We are speechless.

# Dash

*Longer please!*—two out of fifty usable words
you employ to hold us hostage—

longer in the cooling bath, longer
by the playground gates, mowing imaginary grass,

longer driving your car-cum-aeroplane—
and we want longer too—

and smaller boxes to fold your clothes into
or not to have to shed them at all—

but before we know what's hit us,
we're standing on the roadside, staring west

at the last of a trail of dust, like the crowds
who wait all day for a royal visit

for it to simply pass them by—
before they've memorised the hair, the eyes,

the inscrutable footmen, the marvellous horses

# Electric Edwardians

They're here to make money, the men distinguished
from the crowds they move among
by white hats and walking sticks,
to capture as many people as possible
for their fairground bioscope shows.
*Come see yourselves on the screen as living history!*

And history sets up its Nordenograph and rolls
and vacuums in the girls in shawls, the men and boys in caps,
the entire rollicking sea
of spinners and doffers and little tenters
departing the factory gates at six
like a nation's exodus.

Everyone wears clogs. Everyone has a dinner to get to.
But the dock of a quarter-day's pay for a minute of horseplay
is no longer over their heads
and so they jostle, momentarily, blurred face by blurred face,
to smile or to bow, for the transmission of grace
in the space near the cinematographer

as though the camera cast out a fraught pool of light
in exchange for their imprint
and they are standing in it.
The women loiter less. A handful of men doff caps, then laugh
or shake incredibly white, wide handkerchiefs
at whoever may prove their witness:

themselves, their wives, coal miners, tram conductors,
Boer War veterans, Lloyd George in the wings—who knows—
the King—not to mention the unthinkable yet-to-be-born,
not to mention me. And always,
in every factory-gate frame,
like an offering up of driftwood

out of the indeterminate mass
after its comb and polish
or the crystallisation of salt from a smoky suspension,
children linger longest in the foreground,
shoving, lampooning, breaking the line,
or simply staring back at us, across the lens's promise,

as though we still held Passchendaele in our pockets
and could find a way to save them.
They grin and grin—*not yet, not yet*—
while in a corner of the screen, a cart horse stumbles,
flickers, flashes into darkness
where the cellulose nitrate stock rubbed off inside the milk churn.

# Shadows in Siberia According to Kapuściński

Are upright—
cast not by sunlight but by frozen breath:

we breathe
and are enveloped in an outline

and when we pass,
this outline stays suspended, not tethered

to our ankles
as our sun-shadows are. A boy was here—

fantastically dressed
against the arctic frost like an heirloom glass

in bubble wrap—
he has disappeared into the portico

of himself. Not even Alice,
with her knack for finding weaknesses

in the shellac
of this world, left so deft a calling card.

# Note

'York' is a found poem based on the York Mystery Plays, in which the various guilds of the city were each responsible for writing and performing a play in the cycle. 'And episodes in between with a yet more fabulous cohabiting', and the two final lines, are my own.